THE

UNDERNEATH

Other titles by Christopher Cokinos

POETRY

Killing Seasons

Held as Earth

NONFICTION

Hope Is the Thing with Feathers:
A Personal Chronicle of Vanished Birds

The Fallen Sky:
An Tinimate History of Shooting Stars

Bodies, of the Holocene

ANTHOLOGIES

The Sonoran Desert: A Literary Field Guide
(ed. with Eric Magrane)

THE

UNDERNEATH

POEMS

CHRISTOPHER
COKINOS

newamericanpress
Milwaukee, Wis.

n e w a m e r i c a n p r e s s

Printed in the United States of America

ISBN 9781941561140

Interior design by Rob Carroll
Cover design by Brian Matzat

Cover image © 2017 Tate, London
The Future of Statues by René Magritte (1937)
Oil paint on plaster
www.tate.org.uk/

For ordering information, please contact:
Ingram Book Group
One Ingram Blvd.
La Vergne, TN 37086
Phone: (800) 937-8000
Fax: (800) 876-0186
https://www.ingramcontent.com
orders@ingrambook.com

For event and media requests, please contact:
New American Press
www.newamericanpress.com
newamericanpress@gmail.com

A grave calm bends toward an outbreak of doubt.

– James Tate

We are surrounded by curtains.

– René Magritte

TABLE OF CONTENTS

I. VAST AND FLAT

II. THERE ARE STRANGERS

III. KINSHIP OF THE UNDERNEATH

I.

VAST AND FLAT

HUNTERS AT THE EDGE OF NIGHT

Reader, we are two hunters at the edge of night.
Vast and flat, it goes on darkly.

For our rifles and satchels, our boots of hide and coats of wool
can't courage us to far green gloaming. Not enough

to move us from the broken wall, heads pressed to stone, heads
cradled by arms. Hoplophobe, agoraphobe,

we glance at barrels slung upon our backs, cry, look
to the crossing and fall feckless again to this smooth wall.

O cool stone, what did we think we'd do?
Kill what comes in village squares at night?

Ladle blood from fountains, then
sally to the plains to stalk what we could? We cower

at moonrise, moonset, then at what replaces them, clustered
stars in summer, that sun. Chronophobe and chromophobe:

Do we close our eyes or keep them open?
Would that eyes did something better.

Still, we've come farther than the rest,
those other guilds of twitch and shirk,

novitiates of gephyrophobia, who glubbed in the river;
of somniphobia, who died delirious inside pillows; of trypophobia,

who stepped back bug-eyed from pit to pit.
"Black mouth!" they cried. They fell.

More or less, we felt for them and caressed their grub.
Which brought us here, thank you much. For those afraid

of swallowing, of fire, of sound, of cats, of flowers
—what blossoms in that distance?—and of rain

and of hair, of vomit, of heat and of cold, all those have perished
by what they could not love or what they ran to.

At the edge of night's staked plain, we shiver
against the wall's decision. We have no plan but gasping

fables of these woes—shovels and rubble, tea cups and broth, books
stacked neatly on stairs in the redoubts of our disbelieving kin.

THE FUTURE OF STATUES

The myelin sheaths had broken. Electricity found its way uncomfortably, in a panic, really. Something held (your hand) something cold (frozen peas) on the forehead, this greenest desert. At least there were clouds. Later it would thunder and lightning. Virga's beautiful shortcoming. Then monsoons like spots of time, many perfections of collapse. If the brain is wider than the sky, what do you drive under the day after, sun's 100,000-year-old light on the dash, abstractions of a thrust into the dizzy river the streets become, to be washed away as water gussies the closing surface of itself with trash and foam, the jiggling antenna? Why would the sky, like any decent stare, eat grime and dirt reheated till the beeping stops—if it does—and if the brain is wider than the sky, what do you sit under, throbbing from the store, flat and fractional, concussed, alone? A ceiling? Which is a lid.

The rooms you walk in are made of walls. After the black-out you went to the dining room and sat with your head in your hands, the table's dark grain inside a tree once, cold seeping to the heat of failure. Far away, and for whose while she would not come home. Body remembered. Your library. Your vertigo. Yellow note-pad. A grocery list. Two metaphors worth keeping. Chemical to succor into water by some squalor, the pill factory. Your body remembered. All you knew was that the table had been the inside of a tree once. The white matter was changing, had changed, is, would, like someone with a terrible hangover, but more, you'd be told, the pre-morbid dispositions, everything that you'd done wrong, that had gone wrong, that would of course go wrong, crossing the network of ravines, worlds breaking as you yourself are broken.

YOU'RE A YOUNG GIRL EATING A BIRD

Delicate monster,
your collar is bloody.
Your lace, your audacious hands.
In the bare tree behind you,
all that's next that cannot fly: the Fearful Cuckoo,
the Wide-Eyed Cackle, the Trepidatious
Crested Blather. Feathers tickle your nose, a cloud
of feathers haloed round your round face, pulpy
speckles on your lips, hungry pilgrim. Well, of course,
you're not smiling. You have hardly time to gasp,
to slurp and swallow. To pause
is to terrify yourself.
You should know that we understand.
But also that your dress isn't pretty, brown
sackcloth gussied with cheap trim
soaked in blackbird. Your haircut?
Marmish. Look, we're just being honest.
It doesn't mean that we can't help.
Who will wash your things?
Who will pluck the bones from your cheeks?
Wipe your face and comb your hair

then carry you across the ravine before town?
And who will knock on your family door
to explain it all again? Who else
will fail to watch the door close,
the lamp-lit stone of the house
no warmer than the moon-lit stone of the house?

Screaming night, how father vanishes. Hot hours, trailer. Dirt and grime, how your mother waves as you go before you should. Lover folds in half. That was in a garage. Car that hit you, child, to pavement. Those years-ago pipes that knocked you down, that starred your black, that scrawled symptoms, durations, comforts, disasters, which you read now again and again ellipsis send it's happened again. That winter bed by which you wept, holding her waist, unable to do, and, how, transfixed to die. Tenderness, formerly and formally. Latest lesion, read the phrenologist: "The human body may be compared to a steam-engine, which may be perfect in its construction, but unless the right kind and quantity of fuel is supplied, a full force of steam cannot be generated and consequently the engine will be useless. It is from this absence of harmony...that so many literary men break down."

YOU'RE A MERMAN HANGING FROM A GIBBET

The man who strung you up looked an awful lot like you,
with skin for scales and legs instead of fins.
"Brother," you said, "brother, why are you dragging me from the seaside
boulder where I sit and wait for someone new?"
"To get you to the beach and drag you on the sand,
and I am not your brother."
He dragged you on the sand then hooked your mouth
to haul you through the dunes. "Friend,"
you asked, "Why have you hooked my mouth
so blood makes every word I speak?"
"To get you to the top where we can see the whole of the sea
and you can learn to staunch your queries,
and I am not your friend." You thought, "This
man who stops to show us the whole of the sea
dresses modestly: trousers, boots, felt doublet,
a flat-brimmed hat to keep his face in shade,
so all I see are hands at work tugging the hook from me."
The sun dried your fine blue scales so they shimmered less and less.
The breeze dried your fine blue scales so they shimmered less and less.
"I am ugly and hurt," you cried. "Who will want me?"

"Come, come," he said, "it's not so bad. To show you
I will carry you on my back, not to waters where you wallow,
but to my lawn, where near cattails and willows that sway best
     in evening light, where
from my open door painted fresh with diamonds of blue and sun
     and salmon,
I can watch you shimmy after I've noosed and hung you from
     my gibbet."
He was true. The walk was slow, and what slickness you had left
oozed into his shirt to make a stain as dark as your tight eyes.
Your fin slapped his rear, a final shame and stirring.
"Man," you glubbed, specks of blood sprayed upon his skin,
"who says he's not my brother, who says he's not my friend, I know
you well. I remember. How every symptom
makes me sicker than I am, how every lust makes me sadder
than it should. How many times
have you hung me from your gibbet?"
"Counting is like crying," he whispered, "and let's begin with one."

Like a cage, healer an hour of 100,000 months. Twelve voices play each day as you stretch on one floor with two eyes closed trying hard to feel one thing: your left big toe, say, or how every part of your body is held by earth. There are 2,000 birds you should feed, three cats you do. Limbic neuronal attrition, maladaptive pop-up response. Screen. Only three month thread into the ball cap 15 keys, your wallet, your phone before bed. Daily call from her whose while in which day and day. Maybe never. Maybe book that tries to read. Quiet throbbing that drives to store and back, the rain revived is collapse reprised Dr. Year, Dr. Never: Driveway, listen—earth took from earth earth with woe. Earth drew other earth to the earth. Earth laid in an earthen grave. Then earth had of earth enough earth and left the hole alone.

THE DIFFICULT CROSSING

So which are you? Are you
the mold-clouded ceiling?
That iron bar or its dusty curtain?
Which part of this is you?
The pink floor or the steps from the pink floor?
The table with its human leg
or the leg itself, the thin leg
of some chalky girl?
Are you the mannequin's hand
or the crimson dove that it holds down?
"You? You?" calls the dove. Can you
be both desire and thing desired?
Holder and held? Hope
for metaphor and the failure to find it?
The baluster eyeball
unblinks a wall and so can see only
sidelong the far portal to sea,
sheeted blackblue sky, the storm's wave
-crest lightning. It's there
the black ships list, where more queries
of less subdued relevance

sink. You count
three possibilities.
You are a listing black ship.
You are a torn sail.
You're a cold sinew on a watery plank
looking to a room
that doesn't pitch and fold,
where there's a curtain you could crawl beneath
till someone comes to find you.

(What is everywhere that hasn't learned to sing?) Curtains, cover
windows. Walls, there's a ceiling. Car, blare of desert sun everyone.
Finch that hit the window by the feeder didn't fill, trails in dust. Slow
wake mornings. The sink. The kitchen. Plate. Dismal wet stomach is
dismal. Wet heat pavement's swerve and bump, reminiscent ditch.
Eyelids grateful for, sudden, on your belly the weight that makes you
weep, that cat. Is very long before and after she is still there! You get her
from the bus. As well, mail stares. Hinges of metal, maybe never sits in a
chair. Here's a little pie since you've been asking for some. Here's a little
pie since you've been asking. Here's a little

pie. Door, click closed. Axon panic, please just click it. Your library of every last time. Kinds of heads, there are all kinds of heads but all of them are round so thoughts can change direction. Many engines and with wires, how long have you been still or, to put it another way, how long have you been moving? Itch of the cuff. Man who listens, woman who wants less of more. Finger followed by eye tap the knee. Prick of the shin. Walk, line, we think all danger fled, but if the sky is round, the party was loud. Bend spinning to your shoes to gather your aphorisms to crutch you down the street. You've been undone again by 1) her fear; 2) two people talking at once; 3) that Smith's song; 4) a shopping cart; 5) the vacuum cleaner; 6) all of the above. Count how many quizzes your hands can quiver if the drape is deeper than the sea

YOU'RE A PERSON MEDITATING ON MADNESS

How else to explain the luggage,
full or empty, flying from every home
into the caverns, whirling
like fire ash as bats dodge
corners and handles, and every stream
that's running backwards? Hum the sad sounds
the drying fountains make.
Record the lake that drops from knees
to ankles, soles beneath
the creepy dusks of reservoirs.

Machines may yet be crafted, odd
crankshafts and greasy stanzas, large
fans and hasty viaducts.
What burns down close to skin stinks and it hurts.
Okay? Okay. Just watch
how winds draw in
every useless paper, the white and inky cyclone
in which every useless creature
writes a last aubade to finally giving up—

TO COMPANIONS OF FEAR

are one million heads.

Birds of a canyon.
Vulture of birds. Dove of birds.
Sleeping owl and the foliation of its fellows.
Swift and poor will,
black dart passing
clouds as white as trazodone.

Who knows how | they love their dirty talons—

Pull back drusy mountain sun
and there are milligrams of fuse.

For axons have broken you have snapped their tangly make-do.
Little bird brain going wrongly white inside | coax the leafy owls
from greeny nests
before the aphids crawl.

and what is that ocean in the sink? Right prefrontal cortex. The brain
keeps moving (hypochondriac) after the skull has stopped, a point of
contact twice then, the collision outside and the collision inside and
this is how the myelin sheaths—water, lipids, proteins that usher signals
from nerve to nerve—are stripped. The axons themselves do snap. The
brain stutters, then things grow back. It takes time. All your body's
strange return and day by her lake, grassy drives, sorry together a tender
trying hard to feel just one thing, your left sweet sweet because, say.
Little cell it's | frontal and temporal | it's hypometabolism | it's attention
task alteration | even in acute if mild, cerebral substrate

OF CELESTIAL MUSCLES

I. Amygdala: After the Failing Mantra "Worry Does Not Fix the Future"

"Dear little nut,
one warm hand
is on the belly, another
on the chest. Breathe."

But when you close your eyes
to see a weave of trees the branches
are roots that splinter.

Look again
to a day-lit wall whose quivers
you can't detect. A paradox

with viscera would finer be
a paradox without.

II. Hippocampus: Wake

This is new.

Dusty oleander.

Beefy hoots of doves. Morning's mind as

slanty texture of bricks' soft shadows. Morning's mind as

leaf lace in the courtyard.

Now the hunt for each sensation

      to decide what pain you might be in

      —tingle, ache and twitch.

Smell of cat piss baking on the fence. Some engines.

      To decide what pain

      then careening forward, pitched

as that swallowtail dollops eggs

      to stupid lists and unhappened disasters

      you believe is living

on the potted kumquat by your study.

      You miss the mountains, the river, the raspy junipers

      from years before. You miss your mind

      before vial, scan and dose.

      Your body sets aside its

      motive for praise, which you also miss.

On roofs beside acacias, swamp coolers rattle in the desert heat.

The background hum is still quite generous.

So belly down. Scootch close to that thorn tipped with June.

III. *Prefrontal Cortex: Affix*

Pink canker on the cat's chin.

Eloquence of a thrasher. A jet that drags its rancor.

The blossom floats on a pool's water,

and the shadow of the blossom traverses its bottom.

You expect a turn. There is none. You expect torque.

There is none. You expect epiphany, catharsis, retrofits.

There are none. Offering, bulwark, break or breakthrough.

No and no

canticle

but cicada

but finch!

but emptiness. Unholy. Unto. How only

by some easy tension

the petals' wings affix.

Because October here is summer, October is your face. Clouds, cross
your face. Your face is sky. It's too much summer to you roll backwards
100,000 backwards to barely walk head from side to side. Heat hang,
you cannot stand. Well, you stand. Barely read. Book, you can't you cry.
Your face. Your try. You can die sure less than sky, more than brick
than cannot sleep. You, you sleep, queasy citalopram, placid trazodone,
dizzy zolpidem, quiver dizzy cuts to dose the roll to bed. You can't.
Tell her. A test! Walk, tell her, titrate thinner, shed and sallow, hands
on walls you should thank. Thank you walls. Thank you cats. And the
beeping stops...What I hear you saying is...thank you walls thank you
cats...trapped in amber? and she, less and less whose while wires a smile
is less and less of the leap from your ridge without birds,

you, a bird full of trees becoming your left big toe, as if your life depended on it, which, of course, it does, death mask made of cloud-crossed sky, little mariner, could you lengthen out your pain or just drop your awareness into it, to be curious, what does pain feel like? It doesn't feel like wisdom, and screaming erotic songs right now won't help, but breathing might. We all know how to breathe, and the air is moving across the gateways of your nostrils daylight and moonlight the body's strange return the body's very strange return slowing air in the room thus wrecked may light up your thigh over the smooth floor like any decent stare that was a child, knees in chest, and the brain is the organ of the mind, o sublime science, o this faculty, it's as big as the sky like space itself so when you notice that your mind is no longer on the breath why then | you're already back

the difficulty | being, having returned to yourself | that you are left with yourself.

II.

THERE ARE STRANGERS

HAUNTED CASTLE

That evening

    when lightning

        succumbed to stone,

    became stone, you

turned,

    gasping, "Finally

        —I can use this chisel

    to carve your likeness

from the storm."

PERSONAL VALUES

Wherein giant comb leans on cloud-clotted sky, balanced on the bed. You never pull the sheets down. Whisper so it doesn't fall with such long fangs at you. The pill is huge! Nibble and num! The color of cinnamon, so swallow, go ahead, crawl on up, give it a hug, a tilt, a little tongue. You used to like to play. That match on the rug is as long as you, if you had no legs and yearned for exploration. And there's a long-stemmed, blue-green glass, the color of a place and as tall as a mountain tree. There is, atop your wardrobe, the anachronism of a shaving brush. Sometimes you pull the big thing down and crawl inside, breathing like some other creature among its many hairs. When you emerge, the mirror throws you back. That's what mirrors do.

THE LOVERS

Before they kiss, the lovers swathe
their heads in fine white gauze.
They kiss through rocks
he kicked off cliffs
when she said nothing at all.
They kiss through doors
of last year's flat. Through quite-shut
eyes, the sloping back.
Screams not heard above the current black
and, at dinner, a fork set down with an angry tap.
Head in clammy hand, through that,
through headache, through vertigo and plans.
Through broth. Lozenge. Table cloth.
White, raised expressions of leaf.
They kiss through sheets she kicked off
after lock click, notes, ignition.
Failures of prudence and courage.
That stupid song. Patience. The long walk
to another room with books and wind-up toys.
They kiss and scrape through other mouths,
    tongues that taste like tulle.

You know—
You still love—
You misunderstood—
You regard in memory—

WHAT DO YOU OWE THE MAGICIAN'S ACCOMPLICE?

You used to lift the iron gates
and go down into the vaults.
You're a boy playing
in the empty cemetery
with that girl again.
Earth and limestone:
That she smelled what you did
bewildered your stone-stippled palms.

You climbed out. Regained
the light. Saw a painter
by broken
columns, heaped-up leaves.

She'd descend from a golden
stagecraft tube in a room
of mountain walls to be
divided. Her spine and golden hair,
her shoulders emerging
always elsewhere

to watch the naked rest of her
lowered in red thread, accomplice in a wizard's net.

When she took your hand beneath black pleats
she tongued the mild air.

The light regained was sheer amber.
The vaults tested sky
stayed dark stayed quiet.
You ambled a long time somewhere.
Stone and grass brushed
the achromatic shades
and haven't stopped.
How could she? You were autumn. She still is.

MAN OF THE SEA

Is this the kind secret?

Either you're guilty

and have stolen nothing

or you're innocent,

clutching the loot.

YOU'RE TIRED OF LISTENING TO THE GIANTESS

October
and the giantess
still occupies
the dusty corner
speaking ad nauseam
about her trip to California.
You're about to sleep
when she begins to shave
her legs and sex
which is the size
of a lorry full of typewriters
for the armless. Her hairs
fall like god's eyelashes
which you gather up
and brandish toward
the gloomy sequoias.

USE OF SPEECH

Plumed quail:
Curved darkness quivers
on expeditions to the brick ledge
of a curving street named, stupidly, Lester.
You see the monitory, manic pecking
where you plucked
and split on the barrel
cactus hooks the yellow fruits
of the cactus, the

splice, sever, spill that
left the seeds to beaks,
black seeds like black sequins
you slide your finger in
a husk, watch them peck

as you lick, as bite
crisp and lemon and pepper,
your own hunger.

Be cordial, bargain.
Tiny mandibles, little coos.

sky   *human bodies (or forest)*
curtain   *front of the house*

EMPTY MASK, YOU SHOULD HAVE SNAPPED ITS NECK

Mockingbird, ashiver by the curb, wing

akimbo, bolus of organs

worming from its beak

beneath filigrees of leaf.

You looked for a rock, a boot, a mallet, a very heavy cloud.

At helpless doors you looked. You

wagered stripping off your shirt

to wrap it while your hands bore down.

Why not walk home

for a cloth, a shroud

to cover its eyes, something

for your slow hands

to craft a thoughful fracture?

GOLCONDA

You're a well
-dressed man
floating in the sky
with others
of your kind
black slashes
exclamations
without dots.
Altitude is one trench
and placid windows their
furious repose
of tiny difference.
Throaty silence
scores
the calm
the black wool
and shiny abacus
abscess
above angles
and vacant ledgers.
This plaza is ruined
by preference, a legion

of answers to account

better as questions.

What will light

the stones

if you stay here

through the dizzy night?

Can you fetch

the lost sparklers

from the dark green

yard inside your valise?

Having made

the model clipper

by the dogwood

window, having sat

on that ledge, one

of thousands,

can you ask for help?

Who will gesture—will you—

to return every cat

put down with needles

in every stoic youth?

You're a boy again

snipping paintings

from the book you stole.

You're a boy

on a sofa
with plates of Bosch.
Where in the square below
can you finally kiss
your mother's tiny wave?
Look up
at this well
-ordered sky, blue
broken
with men.
Scrutinize
their hats, conjure their
plans to pilfer
coats watch fobs their memoranda
should cobblestone
hold you up.
All the lucky staff
of the perfect
sound are humming
at a distance. Feel
the air behind
their lips. After all:
What designs
for the elegant
echo, the lost columns?

To plunge
if you could
wind would blossom
the tails of your coat
like the skirt
of a bony meter
who pronounces *sorry*
like an ode.

for Joshua Marie Wilkinson

THE BODIES OF ISLE ADAM

Flame crackles back sky, sea-blue cloud. Cloth drapes the balcony you could live on but only step. You watch though to watch empties you: The first is always blank. Second: Sky-skinned, globe and petals, deportment to be noticed by wish. Dances dove hand, rose hand that makes you sad, makes you think | empty to think | emptied to the first and all the blood years touch the air. If you could, well—fuck the air.

THE THREATENED ASSASSIN

So much to ask that you won't answer. Slide

slowly the pocketed poem across the floor

or, by the coat-draped chair, fetch it from your fine valise.

Show us slowly the hand that creeps from sleeve.

Show us your hands that do so well

since made from turning and turning made. The song?

They just stand there—Oafs Like Us—

the mountains old and wrinkled they don't bleed.

We'll take the poem. What Have You Done?

We'll lower our clubs, this net.

We think she sang the song with you.

We think she wrote the poem you took.

Will you bleed the poem and sing the needle, can you staunch the blood?

We're turning for her sound but it's your sick voice that makes us now.

BETRAYAL OF IMAGES

Of course you're in a bar when this man comes up.

He hands you this poem.

Or you find it stained by a wet mug,

its glassy ring of bar-top sweat

another perfect o you'll never kiss.

It's dark in here. There are strangers.

It's taken a long time to arrive.

You came by plane, by carriage, you walked.

It's far or right around the block.

Your head alights with absinthe and ale, words half-heard to slur.

Dark sip and song, you're just looking outside,

sitting in a bar, reading this stupid poem.

Who asks for these things? Jesus. What is this?

Then you're nearly done.

Then you get it, it's over.

This is not the poem.

III.

KINSHIP OF THE UNDERNEATH

THE 16TH OF SEPTEMBER

Elegy stood on the porch.

Night came and Night said,
"Here's the moon. Here's the Milky Way.
Here's the shadow of an owl."

Elegy walked on the grass.
Elegy grew chilled standing
in the canyon breeze

that blew the moon down
that tossed the birch leaves
that kept the swallows flying.

Cliché came out,
put a blanket round their shoulders, saying,
"Old Friends."

UNEXPECTED ANSWER

You might think

these are problems

to be solved—crawling

skin, the slump, the stare—

when, in fact, they are flawless

in the kinship of the underneath.

for Michael Sowder

FLOWERS/DITCH

Some iron bells
hang from the necks
of splendid horses.
They sing from harness,
sleigh and carriage.

Some iron bells
sprout like dangerous plants.
They wand cradle,
dangle air.
Without sound, they sound

the edge. These bells

grow from leaves
with the silence
of things that grow.
Very much a quiet blister.
Sweet lesion.

The moon that's full
is only half, but the bell
that sounds
is neither, both and has.

Like a picture that decides
to unhang, like a nail
that changes its mind, April
quiets its recent harangue.

THE ANNUNCIATION

This desert morning you befriend your grief.
You give it lukewarm peppermint tea
in the shaded courtyard. You don't tell it
to forget, exactly, but
to pay attention, not
to like all things but
to dislike nothing.

> You'd walked the path among those rocks and reached the dusty
> trees
> Where white lattice work looms, sheet of metal muscle, iron
> corrugation
> Studded with bells or slotted cells, affixed to tissue, the restless
> pavilion.

Look, this is the star
-burst now, age of hydrogen
instead of far tomorrow's withered protons, cold
drifted gloom of the universe. You sip.
The river you lost
isn't missing.

What is this current?

> Like symptoms or simpletons, two pawns taller than trees attended the
> pavilion.
> Beyond all that, you saw the land that fell to some abyss, clouds
> Too low and puffed with late-spring rain.

Pipping verdin. Lizard head
-first on the window screen, wide
white mouth of a one-day flower
on a cactus you can't name.

> It was going to drizzle but this pavilion was in no sense a place
> of refuge.
> First you saw the structure as terrifying, as what you are inside, the place
> for what it
> Is: neural totem, rounded forms as nervous fragments, insoluble
> code.

You loved the horsetails by the water years ago.
So old! Before the age of flowers! Spore-topped,
dark green and black, horsetails grow
in a tall white pot your lover set out,
roots and dirt and rocks: a gift, an admonition.

: Formulae for your passage through time and space.

    You saw this.

And finally you understood. It was even lovely. The annunciation

    of terror,

Even as a neural interval stood there, a scan like architecture

    in the timescape of a skull.

AFTER THE WATER,

a mirror mirrored in a pond beneath the room of air and air of else, which is four skies, which is rich, almost shamefully generous, indeed hospitable and very kind, four skies! As if the world had this house, and, like an ancient, takes you unsuspicious to stay for need, to sup when hungry, to sleep when weary, to tell, only when you're ready, such tales of the way that brought you and the way to take tomorrow. This evening, why not pluck the pond's white wood and carve yourself a flute? Why not be an instrument for the house of the world?

MEDITATION

Lungs make light from air.
Tonight all symbols
come home,
and beneath the dark lake
there's a sun whose glow
could reach the shore
if only you rowed
a skiff to the farthest
water and broke the dead
crust of leaves.
That light can light
the snaking candles of the shore,
above the spine, so afraid
of wrinkle, waste and loneliness.
They slither fast to crevice,
but shouldn't.
Rot is its own good smell, your
oar a hand that sweeps
black leaves to stir black water
with its own light.
The match struck, the wicks
hot, the snakes still
and breathing.

BETWEEN

I. Museum

The dust storm swept toward the city, a range-effacing cloud of lifted ground. Black curtain. Lightning. The teacher could have looked. "'The body is a museum of organs,' Jung claimed." The pupils had left, and she closed her mouth, the tongue already dry, legs and arms shaking as one phantom limb. Her lately acknowledged eagerness crackled with sulfurous grains.

II. Rubble

He slept each night with the golden cat crooked in his left arm. Mornings, it hurt to sling the rifle over his shoulder. His wife said nothing. When he died, he'd been moving along tree line. She threw bottles and stones at the cat, but it returned, found her huddled in the tub, walls gone. For one night, they slept together, almost winter.

III. Shovel

A man cleared his way from shack to road, snow flayed like skin pinned back. Silence. In his pocket, a biscuit. He kept shoveling, slicing the snow, tugging on the longest spine. The sky stayed smoke, black mountain of blacker shafts. He dug toward one cobbled village, then another, another, making the path that is no path. This man, he was strong, dying, full of despair, possessing a fine despair the snow in soft piles could not help but wish for.

ELECTIVE AFFINITIES

Broken cornice by another shore.

Tree that opens its door.

Allowing you, on every river, to write the names from every map.

On every map to pour the rivers of the world.

(Once, you walked there, alone among the wild herbs.)

Like a cloud, like a tree, like a house, like all the things we see.

The balloon that lands on a spout.

Black country, wet gown.

Those hours underwater, but also the astonishing discovery of fire.

There is an egg inside the cage.

When it cracks, lift the hook from the eye.

AMOROUS VISTA

Discomfort's door
to someone else,
sadness full of south's
broken compasses.
Panic carved a hole
you walk through.
She's beneath
a single leaf so tall
it shadows sand, shadows
rooms she sketched to live in.
Bell sounds. Sea cymbals.
You find her head
in hands and do not move
till she lifts the vista
that was very tired
that is newly the

 for Kathe

THE BLOOD OF THE WORLD

The desert grows darker then brighter.
The moon clears snags,
and things in the mountains
and things in the valley
grow daggers from their hardy skin.

They're not meant for you.
Only, they are meant for you
if you commit some fault,
and if your feet could be everywhere,
everywhere would be the dangerous
marks of questions preceded
by the blood of the world.

Why are you flayed apace upon
thorns of mercury light,
acacia claws of the underneath?
Why are you always missing
someone you do not know?

You gain a former shore, this desert, peeled
to shavings by your latest journey:

If you were a microscope
perhaps you'd understand better
the branches of plasma
the trees inside pumping undulant
red and black, proteins folded proper

or proteins' folds misplaced. Receptors
hosting or hostile, reuptakes promiscuous
and puritan, patterns nearly geologic
of shapes everywhere, inside as out, waiting
for what they're made to do or, now, made

to do better: Swallow daily to sing more sweetly
in the pump and surge and synapse of it, the head
in hands now legs crossed with ease,
in leisure or restless invitation. Strength
returns as connotation does. Your lens.
That's a paradox. That you become yourself
more and more by saying these strange things.

Walk high enough | and thin and thin and thin the thorns do go.

MUSINGS OF A SOLITARY WALKER

You know you float behind you.
Your naked body a stiff cloud
laid out in air. You walk ahead
in dark clothes
beside a dark river
into the night-time thrum of summer trees
toward that bridge across the water.
The skin behind you smooth, moon-lit polish.
This sounds bleaker than it is.
Once you grant that, you feel your feet
inside shoes as they press down, cold
on wet grass, soft sod.
No one else can see this.
You can't resent your company. How else would it be?
Breath and crackle
of neurons and the night's
lungs humming,
letting others know
that here they are.
Doff your warm hat.
Water creeps across your scalp.
For beads appear, as from nothing.

INTIMATE JOURNAL

Still, sometimes,
you are a man of stone
in a stone world
able only
to carry boulders
to quarry
your heavy body
to carve your face
to shoulder the dawn
while you hold
a valise either
made only of stone
or empty and waiting
to be filled with stones
to be loaded with those
of the morning or those of the night.

NOTES

All the poems take their inspiration from paintings by René Magritte, utilizing the original titles of the works in translation, often in a variant of my making.

The James Tate epigraph is from his poem "Tall Trees by Still Water" in *Constant Defender*.

"The Future of Statues"...some sources, inspirations, allusions: Emily Dickinson, Daniel Parker, Francis Picabia, Bravig Imbs, William Cowper, Geoffrey Grigson, Kenneth Allott, Emanuel Carnaveli, Saburoh Kuroda, David Gascoyne, R.B.D. Wells, René Magritte, James Tate, *Science News*, *Archives of Physical Medicine and Rehabilitation*, *Journal of the International Neuropsychological Society*, *Brain*, *Psychosomatics*, *The Journal of Neuropsychiatry and Clinical Neurosciences*, Jon Kabat-Zinn, The Weakerthans, and a 14th century English verse.

"Wake for the Hippocampus" alludes to a line of Mark Strand's.

"What Do You Owe the Magician's Accomplice?" alludes to Magritte's childhood memory of seeing a painter in a grave yard.

"The Annunciation" cuts in altered prose from J. G. Ballard's essay on Magritte's painting.

"Elective Affinities" uses lines from Magritte and from Verlaine and alludes to the suicide of the painter's mother.

ACKNOWLEDGMENTS

I would like to thank Susan Briante, Michael Sowder, Ben Gunsberg, Fred Marchant, Carolyn Wright, Joshua Marie Wilkinson, Charles Waugh, Jennifer Sinor, and Kathe Lison for their help and various kindnesses with this manuscript. Kathe, I love you.

I'm especially grateful to Gabriel Gudding for selecting this collection for the 2016 New American Press Poetry Prize. Both Okla Elliott and David Bowen at NAP have been fantastic editors and supporters. Many thanks to them and the entire New American Press community. In memoriam, Okla Elliott.

Gratitude to the following publications for presenting my work:

Artful Dodge | "The Threatened Assassin"

Berkeley Poetry Review | "You're Tired of Listening to the Giantess" and "Empty Mask, You Should Have Snapped its Neck"

december | "The Difficult Crossing"

Deep Ends: The J.G. Ballard Book 2015 | "The Annunciation"

District Lit | "Intermission" ("Between")

Jelly Bucket | "The Lovers," "Personal Values," "Haunted Castle"

New Delta Review | "The Blood of the World"

Proximities | "After the Water, the Clouds" ("After the Water,")

Saltfront | "Flowers of the Abyss" ("Flowers/Ditch")

Saranac Review | "Betrayal of Images"

Sugar House Review | "The Amorous Vista"

The Volta's video series Arroyo Chico | "Prefrontal Cortex: Affix"

Western Humanities Review | "You're a Merman Hanging from a Gibbet" and "You're a Young Girl Eating a Bird"

ABOUT THE AUTHOR

CHRISTOPHER COKINOS is the author of *Hope Is the Thing with Feathers: A Personal Chronicle of Vanished Birds* and *The Fallen Sky: An Intimate History of Shooting Stars*, both from Tarcher/Penguin, as well as *Bodies, of the Holocene* (Truman). He is co-editor of *The Sonoran Desert: A Literary Field Guide* (University of Arizona), and his work has appeared in such venues as the *Los Angeles Times*, *Poetry*, *Orion*, *Berkeley Poetry Review*, *TYPO*, *Terrain*, *Pacific Standard* and elsewhere. Winner of awards from the National Science Foundation, the Whiting Foundation, and the Rachel Carson Center for Environment and Society in Munich, among others, Cokinos teaches at the University of Arizona and divides his time between Tucson's Barrio Libre and Logan Canyon, Utah.

www.ingramcontent.com/pod-product-compliance
Lightning Source LLC
Chambersburg PA
CBHW022040090426
42741CB00007B/1137